GAYLORD F

Math Matters!

Size

Look out for these sections to help you learn more about each topic:

Remember...
This provides a summary of the key concept(s) on each two-page entry. Use it to revise what you have learned.

Word check
These are new and important words that help you understand the ideas presented on each two-page entry.

All of the word check entries in this book are shown in the glossary on page 45. The versions in the glossary are sometimes more extensive explanations.

Book link...
Although this book can be used on its own, other titles in the *Math Matters!* set may provide more information on certain topics. This section tells you which other titles to refer to.

Place value

To make it easy for you to see exactly what we are doing, you will find colored columns behind the numbers in all the examples on this and the following pages. This is what the colors mean:

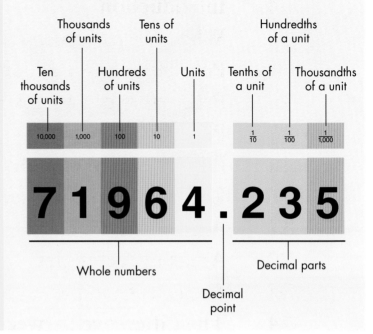

Ten thousands of units — 10,000
Thousands of units — 1,000
Hundreds of units — 100
Tens of units — 10
Units — 1
Tenths of a unit — $\frac{1}{10}$
Hundredths of a unit — $\frac{1}{100}$
Thousandths of a unit — $\frac{1}{1,000}$

7 1 9 6 4 . 2 3 5

Whole numbers

Decimal point

Decimal parts

Series concept by *Brian Knapp and Duncan McCrae*
Text contributed by *Brian Knapp and Colin Bass*
Design and production by *Duncan McCrae*
Illustrations of characters by *Nicolas Debon*
Digital illustrations by *David Woodroffe*
Other illustrations by *Peter Bull Art Studio*
Editing by *Lorna Gilbert and Barbara Carragher*
Layout by *Duncan McCrae and Mark Palmer*
Reprographics by *Global Colour*
Printed and bound by *LEGO SpA, Italy*

First Published in the United States in 1999 by Grolier Educational, Sherman Turnpike, Danbury, CT 06816

Copyright © 1999
Atlantic Europe Publishing Company Limited

Library of Congress Cataloging-in-Publication Data
Math Matters!
    p. cm.
    Includes indexes.
    Contents: v.1.Numbers — v.2.Adding — v.3.Subtracting — v.4.Multiplying — v.5.Dividing — v.6.Decimals — v.7.Fractions – v.8.Shape — v.9.Size — v.10.Tables and Charts — v.11.Grids and Graphs — v.12.Chance and Average — v.13.Mental Arithmetic
ISBN 0–7172–9294–0 (set: alk. paper). — ISBN 0–7172–9295–9 (v.1: alk. paper). — ISBN 0–7172–9296–7 (v.2: alk. paper). — ISBN 0–7172–9297–5 (v.3: alk. paper). — ISBN 0–7172–9298–3 (v.4: alk. paper). — ISBN 0–7172–9299–1 (v.5: alk. paper). — ISBN 0–7172–9300–9 (v.6: alk. paper). — ISBN 0–7172–9301–7 (v.7: alk. paper). — ISBN 0–7172–9302–5 (v.8: alk. paper). — ISBN 0–7172–9303–3 (v.9: alk. paper). — ISBN 0–7172–9304–1 (v.10: alk. paper). — ISBN 0–7172–9305–X (v.11: alk. paper). — ISBN 0–7172–9306–8 (v.12: alk. paper). — ISBN 0–7172–9307–6 (v.13: alk. paper).

    1. Mathematics — Juvenile literature. [1. Mathematics.] I. Grolier Educational Corporation.
QA40.5.M38   1998
510 — dc21   98–7404
                                                      CIP
                                                      AC

This book is manufactured from sustainable managed forests. For every tree cut down at least one more is planted.

Contents

Introduction

$$a = \pi r^2$$

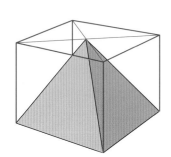

Many things around us come in a wide variety of sizes. In this book you will learn how to measure and work with the sizes of things.

The sizes we use most often are length, area, volume, and angle. For example, we often need to work out the length of an edge of a flat shape. We also often want to know the size of an area inside the shape.

People who are designing and building things need to know how to measure angles accurately.

$$a = \ell \times w$$

$$a = \frac{1}{2}b \times h$$

When we have solid objects like blocks or hollow objects like bottles, we often want to know their volume, or how much they hold – their capacity.

Finding out about sizes has only a few simple rules and some smart tricks that save time and allow us to check our answers.

You will find that by following the stage-by-stage approach of this book, it will be easy to learn how to find out about sizes. Since each idea is set out on a separate page, you can always refer back to an idea if you temporarily forget it.

$$\pi = \frac{22}{7}$$

$$90° + 30° + 60° = 180°$$

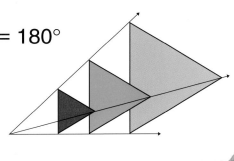

$$v = \ell \times w \times h$$

What is a perimeter?

Think of any shape you like – a piece of paper, a field, the surface of a lake, or a country – each of these things has a line marking its edge. This is the boundary of the shape. Mathematicians call the length of a boundary the perimeter. Here are some examples of boundaries and perimeters.

This historic farm uses a fence to mark its boundary. The perimeter is the length of the fence. The farmer might want to find the length of the perimeter if he were thinking of rebuilding the fence, because he would need to know how many lengths of lumber to order from the lumberyard.

This is a running track. The perimeter is made of straight and curved sections. The total perimeter of many international running tracks is **400** meters.

Perimeter

This is the boundary of a block. Joggers who live on the block might want to know the perimeter of the block so that they could work out how many times they have to jog around the block to complete a 1-kilometer or a 1-mile circuit.

Perimeter

This is a map of Norway. The length of the perimeter is over **5,000** km (**3,000** miles). It is so long because the perimeter includes all the ins and outs of the coast.

Remember... The boundary is the edge. It may be straight, curved, or a mixture of both. The perimeter is the total distance all the way around a flat shape.

Word check

Boundary: The line or curve separating the inside of the shape you are interested in from everything outside it.

Perimeter: The size of the boundary of a flat object. It is the distance once around it.

Perimeters can take on many shapes

The perimeter is simply the length of a boundary. This tells us nothing about its shape. In fact, you can find many different shapes with the same perimeter. Here are a few of them. The perimeter in each case is **100** units.

The shape to the right has five straight sides of equal length. It is called a pentagon. Each straight length is the same and is:

20

$$\frac{100}{5} = 20 \text{ units long}$$

This shape to the right is called a rectangle. It has two pairs of straight sides. It is **40** units long and **10** units wide. The perimeter is:

$$40 + 40 + 10 + 10 = 100$$

10

40

The shape below is long and thin. It contains very little space inside it. The perimeter is:

1 + 7 + 7 + 14 + 14 + 10 + 8 + 17 + 6 + 6 + 5 + 4 + 1 = 100

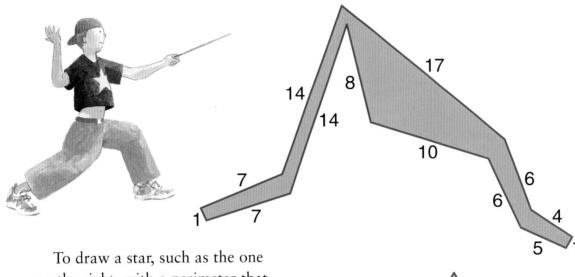

To draw a star, such as the one on the right, with a perimeter that is exactly **100** units, how long must each line in the star be?

To find this out, we need to notice that the star has **20** "rays."

If the perimeter of the star is to be **100** units, then each ray must be ¹⁄₂₀ of the perimeter of **100** units.

$$1 \text{ ray} = \frac{100}{20} = 5$$

But each ray is made up of two lines. So each line of the star is:

$$\frac{5}{2} = 2.5 \text{ units long}$$

These two lines make a ray.

Book link... Find out more about fractions and decimals in the books *Fractions* and *Decimals* in the *Math Matters!* set.

Remember... Many different shapes can have the same perimeter.

Word check
Pair: Two things that match up in some way.

Perimeters of squares and rectangles

Squares and rectangles are straight-sided shapes with four right angles.

In both cases the opposite sides are parallel and have the same length. As a result we can find the perimeter of a rectangle simply by measuring two touching sides and doubling the total.

In the case of a square, because the sides are all the same length, it is even simpler to find the perimeter, as you will see below.

Square

The perimeter of a square is the sum of the lengths of all four sides.
For the square on the right this is:

$$3 + 3 + 3 + 3 = 12$$

However, all four sides are the same length. Remembering that multiplication is a quick way of adding the same number many times, we can write:

$$4 \times 3 = 12$$

Now we can write a formula that allows us to find the perimeter of a square if we know just one length. Suppose the length of the side we know is represented by the letter s, and the perimeter by the letter p. Then the formula is:

The red line is the boundary, or **perimeter** (p), of this yellow square.

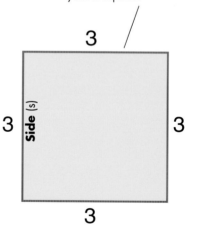

Four times one side equals the perimeter

$$4 \times s = p$$

This could also be written:

$$p = 4 \times s$$

Check that the formula works by putting 3 for s and 12 for p.

Rectangle

The perimeter of a rectangle is the sum of the length of all four sides. In a rectangle the two pairs of sides are of different lengths. In this diagram you can see that one pair of sides is **3** units long, whereas the other pair is **7** units long. The perimeter is

$$3 + 7 + 3 + 7 = 20$$

We have two **3**'s and two **7**'s, so we can write the perimeter as:

$$2 \times 3 + 2 \times 7 = 20$$

Notice that if you were traveling around the rectangle, you would be halfway around when you had completed one short side and one long side.

Suppose the length of the short side is represented by the letter **w** (for width) and the length of the long side by the letter **ℓ** (for length). If we call the perimeter **p**, as before, then the formula is:

$$p = 2\,(w + \ell)$$

This is another way of writing

$$p = (2 \times w) + (2 \times \ell)$$

Check that the formula works by putting **7** for **ℓ**, **3** for **w**, and **20** for **p**.

Remember... A single letter can be used in a formula to stand for a measurement. The formula can then be used again and again with different numbers replacing the letter.

The red line is the boundary, or **perimeter** (p), of this green rectangle.

Width (w)

3

Length (ℓ)

7   7

3

Word check:

Equation: A number sentence using the = symbol, telling us that two different ways of writing a number are the same. For example, 2 + 2 = 4 and 9 − 5 = 4.

Formula: A rule for calculating something. It is often an equation containing a letter or several letters.

Parallel: Parallel lines are lines that will remain the same distance apart forever.

Rectangle: A four-sided shape in which pairs of opposite sides are the same length, and all four corners are right angles.

Right angle: An angle that is exactly a quarter of a complete turn.

Square: A regular rectangle with all four sides the same length and four angles of equal size.

Perimeter of a circle

The perimeter of a circle is called the circumference.

You cannot use a straight edge like a ruler to measure the circumference of a circle because the boundary is curved.

Diameter (d)

Circumference (c)

The red line is the perimeter, or circumference, of the blue circle.

Measuring the circumference

One way to measure the circumference is to roll the circle along a flat surface. You can try this out with a bicycle wheel.

Mark the tire with chalk, and then place the mark against a starting chalk-mark on the ground. Next, roll the wheel in a straight line until the mark meets the ground again. Mark this position on the ground.

Measure the distance between starting and finishing marks on the ground to get the length of the circumference.

Spoke

Mark on tire and ground.

The wheel is rolled in a straight line for one complete rotation until the tire mark meets the ground again.

This length is the circumference of the wheel.

A second mark is made on the ground.

Calculating the circumference

Measuring the circumference of a circle is not easy, and so most people use a simple formula instead. The formula uses the diameter, the distance from one side of the circle to the other.

The formula is:

circumference (c) = **3.14** × **diameter** (d)

It is common to use a small d for diameter and a small c for circumference, so the formula is then:

$$c = 3.14 \times d$$

So, for example, if the diameter of a circle is 5, the circumference is:

$$c = 3.14 \times 5$$
$$c = 15.70$$

You can also use the radius of the circle. Since the radius is half of the diameter, we need to replace the diameter by 2 times the radius in the formula. It is common to use a small r for radius, so the formula is then:

$$c = 3.14 \times 2 \times r$$

Remember... This formula can be used to find the circumference of a circle of any size.

How to use a calculator

Step 1: Enter the diameter (5)
Step 2: Press multiplication sign (×)
Step 3: Enter 3.14
Step 4: Press equals sign (=)
(Answer 15.7)

Note: To find out why we use 3.14 in the formula, turn the page.

Word check

Circumference: The perimeter of a circle.

Diameter: The size of a circle measured straight across through its center.

Formula: A rule for calculating something. It is often an equation containing a letter or several letters.

Radius: The distance from the center of a circle to its boundary. It is half the diameter.

Perimeter and roundness

All circles are the same shape: round. They are just different sizes. You may think this is obvious. But it isn't true for rectangles, triangles, and most other common shapes.

The circumference (c) of a circle is always the diameter (d) multiplied by the same number. The Greeks were the first people to discover this fact, and they called the number pi (π), the Greek for p, the first letter of periphery, which is another word for circumference.

$$\pi = \frac{22}{7} \text{ or } 3.14$$

pi (π) is approximately 3.14 or $\frac{22}{7}$

As a result, you can use either of these formulas:

circumference (c) = **3.14** × **diameter** (d)

or

circumference (c) = $\frac{22}{7}$ × **diameter** (d)

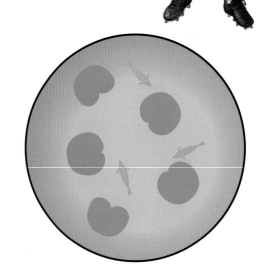

Fenced off

Harvey wanted to put a fence around his garden pond to stop his dog from jumping in it. His pond was 7 meters across. How much fencing did he need?

We know that the circumference of a circle is found by using the formula:

$$c = \frac{22}{7} \times d$$

This time we have chosen the formula that includes a fraction.

Putting the pond diameter into the formula gives:

$$c = \frac{22}{7} \times 7$$

dividing through by 7:

$$c = 22$$

The drum

John wanted to buy enough cord to go exactly around a replica African drum he was making. The cord would be stuck to the drum to make a fine finishing edge.

John designed his drum to be **30 cm** across, so he needed to calculate the circumference of the drum to find out how much cord to buy.

This time we will use the version of formula that includes the decimal number for pi.

Using the formula:

$$c = 3.14 \times d$$

$$c = 3.14 \times 30$$

$$c = 94.20 \text{ cm}$$

This is almost **100 cm** or **1 meter**, and so John needed to buy **1 meter** of cord for each loop around the drum.

Remember... You can use either the decimal number or the fraction for pi in the formula. Use the one that you think will work out most easily.

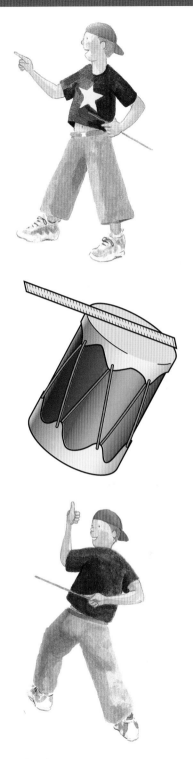

Word check

Periphery: Another word for circumference.

Pi: The number of times the circumference of a circle is bigger than the diameter. It is given a special name because it cannot be written down precisely as a fraction or as a decimal. It is approximately $\frac{22}{7}$, or 3.14159265...

Length of mixed shapes

Many objects are made of straight and round sections. To find the combined length, deal with each type of shape separately, then add the results.

You can see how to do this using the example of a paper clip. A paper clip is made of a single piece of wire bent into round and straight parts

When the paper clip is spread out, you can see the round and straight parts more clearly, as shown on the right.

Total = straight parts + round parts

Step 1: Start with the straight parts. There are four straight parts. Adding them we get:

$$3 + 4 + 2 + 3 = 12$$

Step 2: Next do the round parts. There are three round ends. Each round end is a semicircle – half a circle.

The width of the round end is the same as the diameter. Find the length of the larger round end.

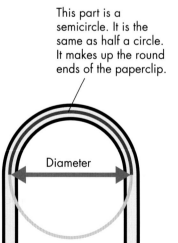

This part is a semicircle. It is the same as half a circle. It makes up the round ends of the paperclip.

Diameter

The circumference of a circle is 3.14 × diameter. The round end is half a circle, so its length is:

$$\frac{3.14 \times \text{diameter}}{2}$$

We have three round ends. They have diameters of 1 centimeter, 0.8 centimeters, and 0.6 centimeters. We put each of these diameters into the formula above like this:

1-cm diameter round end:

$$\frac{3.14 \times 1}{2} = 1.57$$

0.8-cm diameter round end:

$$\frac{3.14 \times 0.8}{2} = 1.26$$

0.6-cm diameter round end:

$$\frac{3.14 \times 0.6}{2} = 0.94$$

Adding these values gives us the length of the rounded parts:

$$1.57 + 1.26 + 0.94 = 3.77$$

Step 3: The total length of the paper clip is:

$$= 12 + 3.77$$

$$= 15.77 \text{ cm} \text{ (nearly 16 cm)}$$

Remember... If you want to find the length of a complicated shape, try to split up your task into easy parts such as straight sections and curved sections.

Book link... For more information on multiplying with decimals see the books *Multiplying* and *Decimals* in the *Math Matters!* set.

Areas of squares

The amount of surface something covers is called its area. Area is used to measure the size of the inside of a flat shape. It might be the amount of carpet you need to cover your bedroom floor, or the amount of turf needed to cover a lawn, or the amount of land covered by a forest, or country or state.

Unit squares and square units

When we measure area, we use square units. First, we draw a square that is one unit along each side. If we are measuring length in inches, the square will be 1 inch on each side. The area of that square is called 1 square inch, often written as 1 in².

If we are measuring length in centimeters, the square will be 1 cm on each side. The area of that square is called 1 square cm, often written as 1 cm².

Calculating areas of squares

To find the area of a square, use this formula:

area (a) = **length** (ℓ) × **width** (w)

$$a = \ell \times w$$

Because every side in a square is the same length, the area is simply any side multiplied by itself.

Finding areas of squares

Each playing square on the chess board in the picture opposite has a side **5 cm** long. We can find the area of one playing square by counting how many 1 cm² squares can be fitted into it.

You can see from the diagram below that **25** of these fit in. We say that the area of the playing square is **25** cm².

8 squares

1 cm

1 cm — **1**

This is a single square. It is 1 cm² in area.

5 cm

5 cm

Each square has a side of 5 cm

Alternatively, we could have found the area by multiplying one side by itself:

$$a = 5 \times 5$$
$$a = 25 \text{ cm}^2$$

which, of course, is far quicker.

Remember... Because a square has sides all the same length, the area is found by multiplying the length of any side by itself.

Word check

Area: The size of the shape within a boundary. It is measured in square units by counting how many unit squares can be fitted into it.

Square unit: The same area as is in a square with sides one unit long. It can be any shape.

Areas of rectangles

A rectangle is a shape with four straight sides and corners that are all right angles. Unlike a square, the touching sides are not the same length.

You can see the difference between a square and a rectangle by looking again at the chess board.

"My half" of the chess board is the four rows at my end. Each row contains eight playing squares. "My half" is a rectangle.

The area of a rectangle is found by the formula:

area (a) = **length** (ℓ) × **width** (w)

$$a = \ell \times w$$

The 4 rows total 20 cm, the 8 columns total 40 cm.

So the area is:

$$a = 20 \times 40$$

$$a = 800 \text{ cm}^2$$

Check your calculation

You can count that I have 32 playing squares in my half of the board. Each one is 5 cm × 5 cm or 25 cm².

You can multiply the number of playing squares by the area of each one:

$$a = 32 \times 25$$

$$a = 800 \text{ cm}^2$$

Length (ℓ)
24 m

Width (w)
11 m

The area of a tennis court

A tennis court is **24** meters long and **11** meters wide.

To find its area, we could cover it with squares 1 meter on each side and count them.

Or we could add **24 + 24 + 24 +** etc., eleven times (or add **11 + 11 + 11 +** etc., twenty-four times), or we could multiply **24 × 11**, which is by far the quickest method.

100	10	1
	2	4
×	1	1
2	4	0
	2	4
2	6	4

The answer is **264** m².

Book link... To find out more about multiplication using columns, see the book *Multiplying* in the *Math Matters!* set

Word Check

Rectangle: A four-sided shape in which pairs of opposite sides are the same length, and all four corners are right angles.

Right angle: An angle that is exactly a quarter of a complete turn.

Remember... Multiplying is a quick way of adding similar things, which is what we are doing when we count areas.

Areas of triangles

One way to think of the area of a triangle is to imagine it as half a rectangle. To understand how to find the area of a triangle, start with a rectangle, like the one to the right, and draw a line between opposite corners (a diagonal).

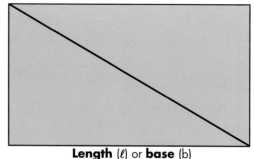

Width (w)
or
height (h)

Length (ℓ) or **base** (b)

Both parts of the rectangle are now triangles, and since both are the same shape and size, you can see that the area of one triangle is half the area of the rectangle. On page 18 we saw that the area of a rectangle (a) is length (ℓ) multiplied by width (w):

$$a = \ell \times w$$

and since the area of a triangle is half of this, the area of a triangle is:

$$a = \frac{1}{2}\ell \times w$$

When dealing with triangles, mathematicians normally use the word "base" for the horizontal side and "height" for the line at right angles to the base.
This means that we write the area as:

$$a = \frac{1}{2}b \times h$$

This formula is always true no matter what shape the triangle.
See how the height divides the rectangle into two pairs of equal triangles, showing that the area of any triangle is half the area of the rectangle.

The shaded part of each rectangle has the same area as the unshaded part.

Height (h)

Base (b)

Areas of triangles with the same base and height are always the same

Two gardeners were arguing over the biggest area of a triangular flower bed. One side had to be the same length as a window, and the flower bed also had to reach to the path. The first gardener said that his broad triangle would have the biggest area, while the second said that a triangle with the longest possible sides would have a bigger area.

Who was right? They were both wrong because the area of a triangle is ½ base × height, as we saw on page 22. The base for both triangles is the window, and since they must also both reach the path, the height of the triangles will also be the same. So, no matter what shape of triangle they laid out, the area would always be the same.

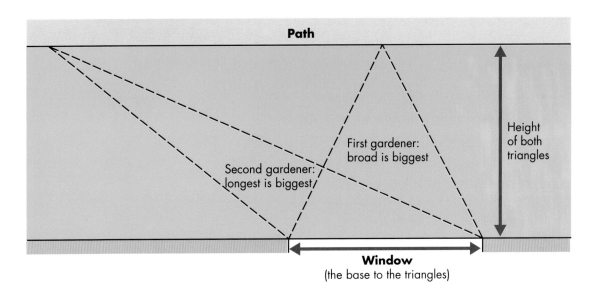

Path

Height of both triangles

First gardener: broad is biggest

Second gardener: longest is biggest

Window
(the base to the triangles)

Remember... The formula:
area of triangle (a) = ½ base (b) × height (h).
The height of a triangle is always measured perpendicularly to the base.

Word Check
Base: The starting line for drawing a triangle.

Parallel: Parallel lines are lines that will remain the same distance apart forever.

Perpendicular: Two lines that meet or cross at right angles are called perpendicular.

The difference between squares

Finding areas can often be done by both multiplication and subtraction.

A new garden

The chief gardener for the city council designed a new pattern of flower beds for the main square. The beds would be laid out using two squares, one inside the other, as shown. The center square would be filled with flowering plants, while the outer triangles would be mountain plants growing in beds of gravel. The assistant gardener had to find out how much gravel was needed for the triangular beds. For this he needed to know the areas of the triangles.

He tried to find the answer in two ways, as described below.

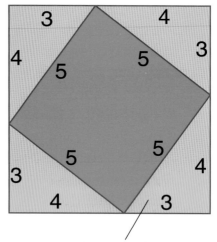

These triangular areas are to be covered with gravel.

Example 1

The design is made from two squares, one inside the other. The area of gravel can be seen as the difference between the areas of the squares:

Area of larger square (a) = length (ℓ) × width (w):

$$a = 7 \times 7 = 49$$

Area of smaller square (a) = length (ℓ) × width (w):

$$a = 5 \times 5 = 25$$

Difference in areas = larger square – smaller square:

$$49 - 25 = 24$$

Book link... Find out more about how to work out the difference between two squares in the book *Mental Arithmetic* in the *Math Matters!* set.

To see why you can subtract areas, the smaller shape has been turned around to show you that it is a simple square.

Example 2

Area of each of the triangles is:

$$a = \frac{1}{2} b \times h$$

$$a = \frac{1}{2} \times 3 \times 4$$

$$a = 6$$

There are four identical triangles, so the total area of the triangles is:

$$a = 6 \times 4$$

$$a = 24$$

The answer in both examples was 24, which could be square yards (yd^2), square meters (m^2), or whatever measure you are using.

5

4 **Height** (h)

3
Base (b)

Remember... When you can use two ways to solve a problem, it is sensible to use both to check the answer.

Word Check

Parallel: Parallel lines are lines that will remain the same distance apart forever.

Perpendicular: Two lines that meet or cross at right angles are called perpendicular.

Mixed rectangles and triangles

Many shapes are more complicated than simply rectangles, triangles, or circles. These are mixed shapes.

To find the area of a mixed shape, draw lines to separate the shapes into rectangles, triangles, or circles.

Next, find the area of each part, and finally add the parts together.

Here is an example.

Painting the garden shed

Tom's dad had to paint the walls of a large shed. To do this, he needed to know the area of the outside of the shed so that he could order the right amount of paint.

We have three shapes in this problem. Let's start with the rectangles. At the back of the shed there is a deep rectangle. Using the formula:

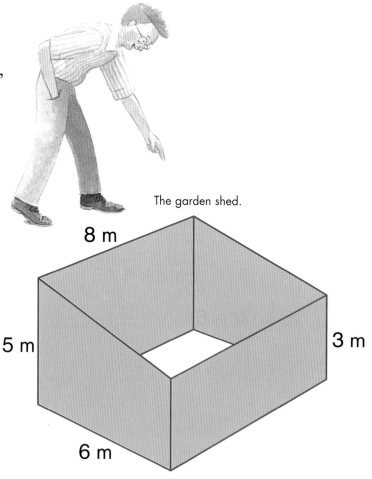

The garden shed.

8 m

5 m

3 m

6 m

$$\textbf{area (a)} = \textbf{length } (\ell) \times \textbf{width } (w)$$

the area of the back of the shed is:

$$a = 8 \times 5$$

$$a = 40$$

Length (ℓ)
8

Width (w) 5

The back of the shed.

At the front there is a shallow rectangle:

$$a = 8 \times 3$$

$$a = 24$$

Length (ℓ)
8

Width (w) 3

The front of the shed.

The sides are more complicated, but they can be simplified into a rectangle and a triangle. First the area of each rectangle is:

$$a = 6 \times 3$$
$$a = 18$$

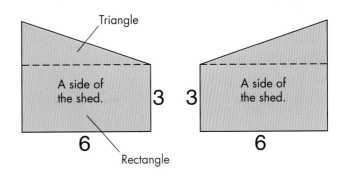

Triangle

A side of the shed.

3   3

A side of the shed.

6   6

Rectangle

Now the area of each triangle.

area (a) = half base (b) × height (h)

The base is 6. The height is the height of the back minus the front height, or $5 - 3 = 2$, therefore:

$$a = \frac{1}{2} \times 6 \times 2$$
$$a = 6$$

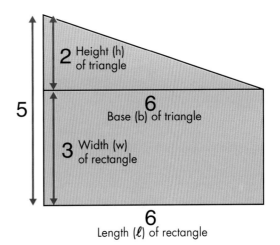

2 Height (h) of triangle

5

6
Base (b) of triangle

3 Width (w) of rectangle

6
Length (ℓ) of rectangle

Therefore the area of one side equals the area of the rectangle plus the area of the triangle:

$$a = 18 + 6$$
$$a = 24$$

Remember, there are two sides, so the area of the two sides is:

$$a = 24 \times 2 = 48$$

Adding sides to the ends gives:

$$a = 40 + 24 + 48$$
$$a = 112$$

All the answers could be in square meters, square yards, or whatever unit you are working with.

Remember... Split up complicated shapes into simpler shapes, then add the results.

Mixed circles and rectangles

The area of a circle can be found using the formula:

$$a = \pi r^2$$

(area is pi multiplied by the radius squared).

Or the formula:

$$a = \frac{\pi d^2}{4}$$

(area is pi multiplied by the diameter squared divided by 4).

Turfing a running track

The groundsman of a running track had to sow a specially hard-wearing new sports grass over the inside area of the track. He needed to work out the area inside the track so that he would know how much seed to order.

To find the area of a running track, split the calculation into two parts. First, calculate the area of the two semicircular ends (two semicircles make a circle). The diameter of the circle is 70 meters. So the easiest formula to use is the one with the diameter in it. In this case we will also choose to use the fraction value of $^{22}\!/_7$ for pi.

$$a = \frac{22}{7} \times \frac{70 \times 70}{4}$$

Dividing through by 7:

$$a = \frac{22}{1} \times \frac{10 \times 70}{4}$$

Semicircular end

Central rectangle

90 m

70 m

Semicircular end

Diameter (d)
70 m

Dividing through by 2:

$$a = \frac{11}{1} \times \frac{10 \times 70}{2}$$

Dividing through by 2 again:

$$a = 11 \times 5 \times 70$$

$$a = 3{,}850 \text{ m}^2$$

The area of the two semicircular ends together comes to 3,850 m².

The area of the central rectangle can easily be found using the formula for the area of a rectangle from page 20:

$$a = \ell \times w$$

The length (ℓ) is 90 m, and the width (w) is 70 m, so the area is:

$$a = 90 \times 70$$

$$a = 6{,}300 \text{ m}^2$$

The groundsman will need enough seed to sow grass on the total area of:

$$a = 3{,}850 + 6{,}300$$

$$a = 10{,}150 \text{ m}^2$$

Remember... Formulas for areas have two length measurements multiplied together:

$a = \ell \times w$ (rectangle)

$a = \pi \times r \times r$ (circle)

Width (w)
70 m

Length (ℓ)
90 m

Volumes of box shapes

The amount of space taken up by something is called its volume. It might be the amount of space in your lunch box, the amount of space in a freezer taken up by an ice-cream tub, or the amount of water in a lake or an ocean.

Volume measures the size of a three dimensional (3D) object, which has a thickness as well as length and width.

For volume we use one cubic meter, 1 cubic foot, or whatever unit we are interested in. It is written m³, ft³, and so on.

Calculating volume

This box is **50** centimeters long, **30** centimeters high, and **40** centimeters wide.

Here is how to find the volume (v) of the box and, at the same time, find a formula for the volume of any object.

The area of the front of the box is:

$$a = 50 \times 30$$

$$a = 1{,}500 \text{ cm}^2$$

If we travel 1 unit back along the width, we could stack **1,500** blocks each 1 cm × 1 cm × 1 cm.

By the time we reach the back of the box, we could have done this **40** times.

So the amount of space taken up by the box is:

$$v = 1{,}500 \times 40$$

$$v = 60{,}000 \text{ cm}^3$$

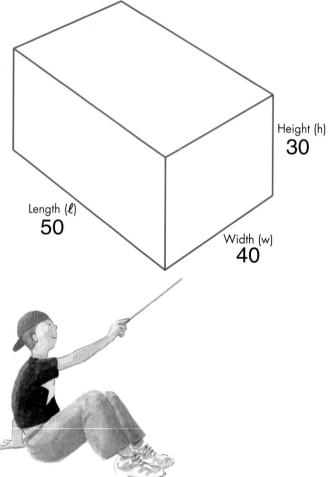

Height (h)
30

Length (ℓ)
50

Width (w)
40

Therefore, the formula for volume (v) is:

volume (v) = **width** (w) × **height** (h) × **length** (ℓ)

Finding the capacity of a freezer

The maximum volume that something can hold is called its capacity. The inside space of a freezer is **70 cm** high, **70 cm** deep, and **170 cm** wide. How much can it hold?

The capacity is:

$$v = \ell \times w \times h$$

$$v = 170 \times 70 \times 70$$

$$v = 833{,}000 \text{ cm}^3$$

There are **1,000** cm³ in **1** liter, so the capacity of the material that could be fitted inside is **833** liters.

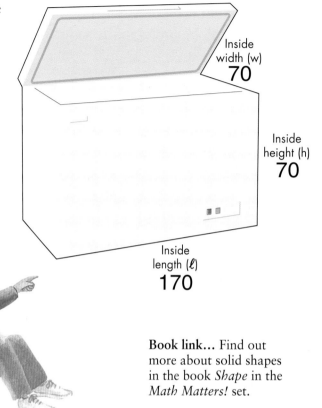

Inside width (w) **70**

Inside height (h) **70**

Inside length (ℓ) **170**

Book link... Find out more about solid shapes in the book *Shape* in the *Math Matters!* set.

Remember... The formula for finding a volume (v) is:
volume = length × width × depth.

Word check

3D: A three-dimensional shape (3D) has length and breadth and thickness (depth). It can be solid, just a surface, or even an open framework, like a pylon.

Capacity: The maximum volume that a container can hold. It is measured in special units such as pints or liters.

Cubic unit: The same volume as is contained in a unit cube. It can be any shape.

Cuboid: A 3D shape with six faces that are all rectangles; some but not all may be squares.

Volume: The size of a 3D shape. It is measured in cubic units (such as cm³ or in³) by counting how many unit cubes can be fitted into it.

Volumes of other solid shapes

The volume of cans and some other containers can be found in the same way as for a box.

Volume of a cylinder or rod

There are many cylinders in your kitchen used as containers for honey, cocoa, and other things.

The formula to use for the volume is:

volume = area of end × length

Area of circular end:

$$a = \frac{\pi d^2}{4} \quad \text{(see page 28)}$$

$$a = \frac{22}{7} \times \frac{14 \times 14}{4}$$

Dividing through by 7:

$$a = \frac{22}{1} \times \frac{2 \times 14}{4}$$

Dividing through by 2:

$$a = 11 \times 1 \times 14$$

$$a = 154 \text{ cm}^2$$

The volume is area of end × length:

$$v = 154 \times 20$$

$$v = 3{,}080 \text{ cm}^2$$

Since **1** liter is **1,000** cm³, this is just over **3** liters.

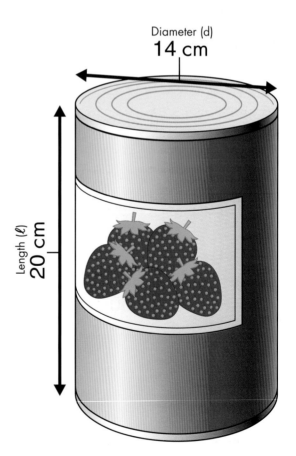

Diameter (d)
14 cm

Length (ℓ)
20 cm

Book link... Find out more about cylinders and other shapes in the book *Shape* in the *Math Matters!* set.

Volume of a pyramid

The volume of a pyramid is exactly a third of the volume of a box that it will just fit into.

In this diagram the height of the box is the same as the height of the pyramid, while the base of the box is the same as the base of the pyramid.

The formula is:

$$\textbf{volume} = \frac{1}{3} \textbf{ of the area of the base} \times \textbf{height}$$

The volume of a giant pyramid

The largest of the pyramids at Giza, Egypt, is called Khufu's pyramid. It is one of the greatest manmade wonders of the ancient world. About one hundred thousand people working part time may have built the pyramid over 20 years.

The sides of its base are 230 m (755 ft) long, and it originally reached 147 m (481 ft) in height.

The volume of the pyramid is:

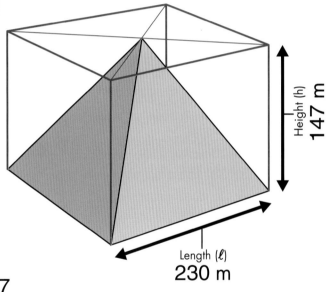

Height (h) 147 m

Length (ℓ) 230 m

$$v = \frac{1}{3} \times 230 \times 230 \times 147$$

$$v = 2{,}592{,}100 \text{ cubic meters}$$

(The stones to make it weighed nearly 6 million tons in total!)

Remember… Volume of a cylinder is: area of end × height.

The volume of any pyramid is ⅓ the volume of the box that it will just fit into.

Angles

A degree is the unit of angle, or turn. The ancient Babylonians invented the use of degrees because they found **60** a very easy number to work with. The Babylonians used a triangle with three equal sides (an equilateral triangle) and divided each of the angles into **60** equal parts. Each of these little angles is called one degree.

If you add 360 degrees together, you make a complete turn.

360 is a very convenient number of degrees to have in a full circle. 360 divides by all of these numbers:

2, 3, 4, 5, 6, 8, 9, 10, 12, 15, 18, 20, 24,

30, 36, 40, 45, 60, 72, 90, 120, and 180.

Dividing a whole turn into equal parts using any of these numbers will produce a whole number of degrees for an answer.

Some common angles are:

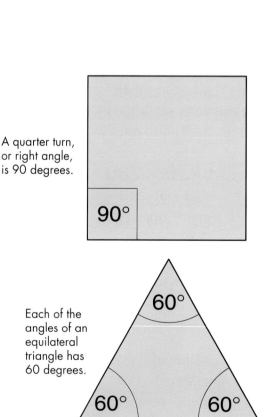

A quarter turn, or right angle, is 90 degrees.

90°

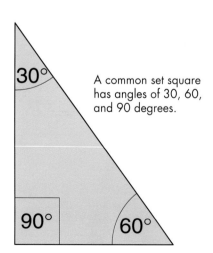

A common set square has angles of 30, 60, and 90 degrees.

30°

90°

60°

Each of the angles of an equilateral triangle has 60 degrees.

60°

60°

60°

Angles are measured with an instrument called a protractor, a measuring instrument marked off in degrees. It can be used to measure or to draw angles.

There are three main types of protractor. The most common is a semicircular protractor, which has a flat base. It has a center point, and its flat base is parallel to a line called a zero line. There are two scales so that you can measure an angle either from the left or the right. Each scale goes from 0 to 180°.

◀ A semicircular protractor

◀ The circular protractor can be used to measure up to a complete turn.

◀ The third type of protractor is called an angle measurer. This is a circular protractor with a moveable arm. To measure an angle with a protractor, line up the zero line along one arm of the angle with the point of the angle at the center of the protractor. Then read the angle on the scale.

Triangles that do a complete turn

Circles, triangles, and the amount of turning are all closely related in a natural way. The natural way to divide a circle is like this:

Draw a circle using a compass. Without changing the separation on your compass, put the point anywhere on the boundary, draw an arc, move the point of the compass to where the arc crosses the circle boundary, and draw another arc. Repeat until you come back to your starting point.

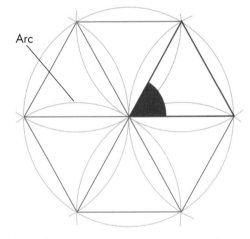

Arc

The red triangle is an equilateral triangle because, using your compass, you made all of its sides the same length. Six of these equilateral triangles make up a whole turn. The angle shaded red between the two red arms is exactly one-sixth of a whole turn. A whole turn is 360°, and so a sixth of a turn is 60°. Thus 60 is a natural unit to choose for measuring the amount of turn.

Book link... Find out more about numbers in the book *Numbers* in the *Math Matters!* set.

Word check

Arc: Part of a circle. It is drawn using a compass.

Degree: A small part of a complete turn. There are 360 degrees in a complete turn. It is shown by the symbol °.

Remember... Although you can divide a complete turn into 360 degrees, the most useful angles to remember are 30°, 60°, and 90°.

How to divide an angle in half

Dividing an angle in half can be
done easily with a compass.

Step 1: Draw the angle you want to divide.

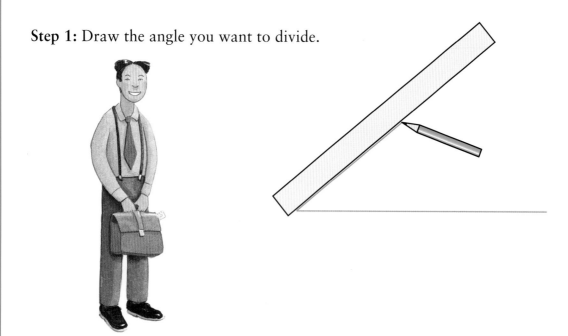

Step 2: Open your compass to any
convenient width, and draw an arc
from the point of the angle O.

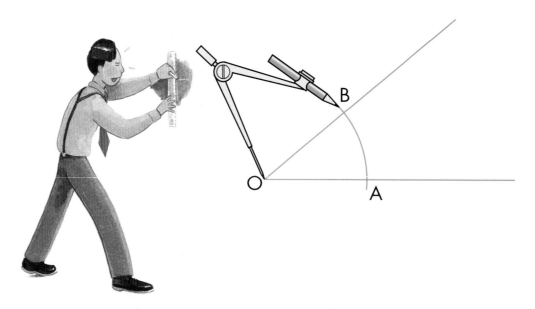

Step 3: Keeping the compass the same width, use points A and B to place the point of your compass. From each point draw another arc.

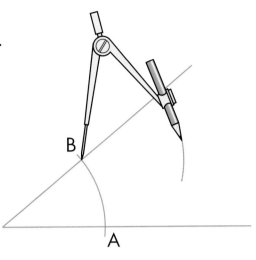

When you have done this, you will find that the arcs cross. On our diagram we have marked this point of crossing as M.

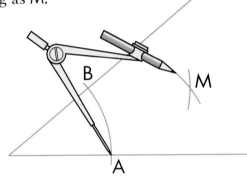

Step 4: If you join point O to point M, you will have a line that divides the angle in two exactly.

The angles of a triangle add up to 180°

One of the most important properties of triangles is that the angles of a triangle add up to **180°**, which is half a complete turn or a straight angle. You can see this by using three identical triangles. In this case we are using a **30–60–90** triangle, but <u>any</u> identical triangles can be used.

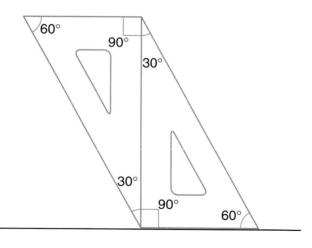

Step 1: Place one triangle on a line drawn on a piece of paper.

30°

90°   60°

This base line is a straight angle or 180°.

Step 2: Place the second triangle so that the 30° angle lines up with the 90° angle of the first triangle.

60°
90°
30°

30°
90°   60°

Step 3: Now place the third triangle so that the 60° angle lines up next to the 30° and the 90° angles.

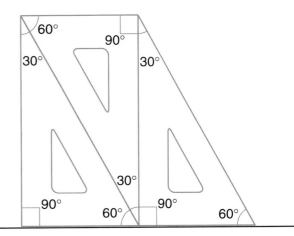

When you put the last triangle in place, its edge lies along the base line, showing that three angles of a triangle add up to half a turn:

$$90° + 30° + 60° = 180°$$

Below is a triangle cut from cardboard. There is nothing special about the angles. Each corner has been cut off and rearranged on a base line. Again they make half a turn, or 180°.

Book link... Find out more about triangles in the book *Shape* in the *Math Matters!* set.

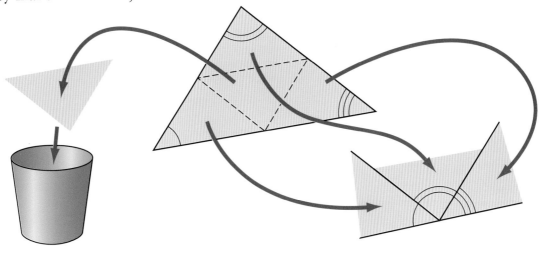

Remember... Triangles come in many shapes. The three angles <u>always</u> total 180°.

Finding the missing angle

The fact that the three inside angles of a triangle add up to **180°** can be used to find the value of a missing angle when two others are known.

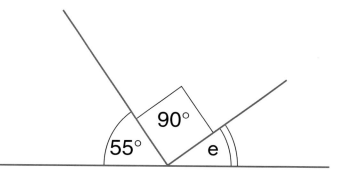

In the diagram on the right you can see that three lines have been drawn so that three angles are formed. Two of the angles are known, but we need to find the size of the third angle.

  We know that a half turn is 180°. So all the angles must add up to 180°:

$$55° + 90° + e = 180°$$

Because:

$$55° + 90° = 145°$$

So:

$$145° + e = 180°$$

  Now, take **145** from each side of the equation:

$$e = 180° - 145°$$

$$e = 35°$$

Here is another example. Find m:

$$57° + 47° + m = 180°$$

$$104° + m = 180°$$

Take **104** from both sides:

$$m = 76°$$

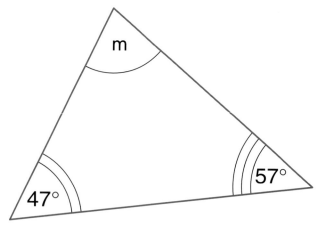

In this example you have been given only one angle. However, the triangle has two equal angles because it is an isosceles triangle. So the other base angle must also be 70°:

$$70° + 70° + p = 180°$$
$$140° + p = 180°$$

Take 140° from both sides of the equation:

$$p = 40°$$

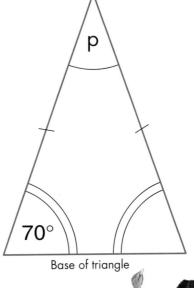

p

70°

Base of triangle

Here is another isosceles triangle. In this case we are given the unequal angle, and we know that the other two angles are the same.

$$2 \times q + 128° = 180°$$

Take 128° from each side of the equation:

$$2 \times q = 52°$$

Now divide each side by 2:

$$q = \frac{52°}{2}$$
$$q = 26°$$

128°

q

Base of triangle

(Check: 26° + 26° + 128° = 180°)

Remember... Always check your answer by adding the three angles together. They must come to 180°.

Word check
Isosceles: A triangle or a trapezium with just two sides the same length is called isosceles.

Enlargement

When you enlarge something, you change its size, not its shape or its angles.

By enlarging an object, all of its lengths are multiplied by the same number.

When you enlarge something, you multiply all of its lengths by a number bigger than 1. If you multiply its lengths by a number smaller than 1, you make it smaller. This is called reducing. Reducing and enlarging are therefore opposites.

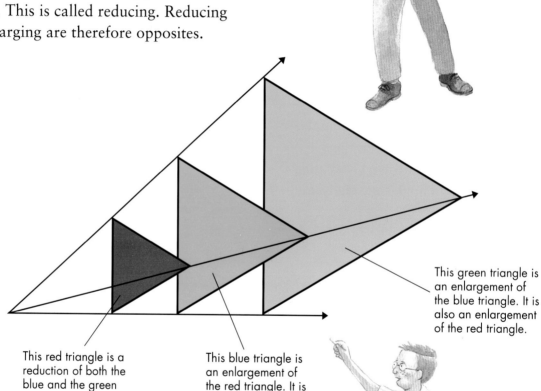

This green triangle is an enlargement of the blue triangle. It is also an enlargement of the red triangle.

This red triangle is a reduction of both the blue and the green triangles.

This blue triangle is an enlargement of the red triangle. It is also a reduction of the green triangle.

Drawing an enlargement

The easiest way to enlarge or reduce something is often to make a scale drawing of it.

Decide by how much you want to enlarge the object. In this case we are going to make a square 2 times bigger, as shown on page 43.

Step 1: Use a piece of graph paper, and draw out the square close to the bottom left of it.

Mark a position in the bottom left-hand corner of the paper. This will be the center from which we make our enlargement.

Draw a ray (a line) from your center of enlargement through all four corners of the square.

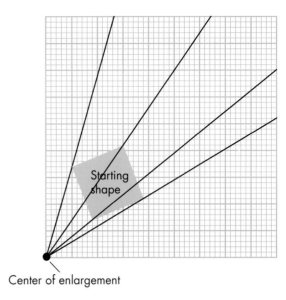

Center of enlargement

Step 2: Select one ray, and measure the distance from the center of enlargement to the corner of the square. Now multiply this distance by 2, and mark a second point along the ray where this falls.

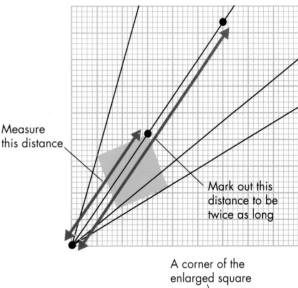

Measure this distance

Mark out this distance to be twice as long

Step 3: Repeat step 2 for all four corners, and mark points twice as far along each ray as the distance from the center to each corner.

Join the four new points to show the enlarged square.

Remember… The easiest way to make a shape bigger or smaller is to use the drawing method.

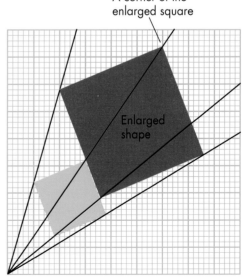

A corner of the enlarged square

Enlarged shape

What symbols mean

Some common geometry symbols together with an example of how they are used:

Right angle (90°)

Curves in angles show that the angle is larger than or less than a right angle.

Angles with the same number of curves are the same size.

Outer line: The boundary of a shape.

Ticks: Lines (sides or diagonals) with the same number of ticks are the same length.

Arrowheads: Sides with the same number of arrowheads are parallel.

Diagonal lines: A line crossing the inside of a shape from one corner to another.

Dashed lines show lines of flip symmetry.

Some common math symbols:

+ The symbol for adding. We say it "plus." In Latin *plus* means "more."

− Between two numbers this symbol means "subtract" or "minus." In front of one number it means the number is negative. In Latin *minus* means "less."

✗ The symbol for multiplying. We say it "multiplied by" or "times."

—, /, and **÷** Three symbols for dividing. We say it "divided by." A pair of numbers above and below a / or − make a fraction, so ⅖ or $\frac{2}{5}$ is the fraction two-fifths.

= The symbol for equals. We say it "equals" or "makes." It comes from a Latin word meaning "level" because weighing scales are level when the amounts on each side are equal.

■ This is a decimal point. It is a dot written after the units when a number contains parts of a unit as well as whole numbers.

( ) Parentheses. You do everything inside the parentheses first. Parentheses always occur in pairs.

% : The symbol for percent.

π : The symbol for pi.

° : The symbol for degrees.

Glossary

Terms commonly used in this book.

Arc: Part of a circle. It is drawn using a compass.

Area: The size of the shape within a boundary. It is measured in square units by counting how many unit squares can be fitted into it.

Base: The starting line for drawing a triangle.

Boundary: The line or curve separating the inside of the shape you are interested in from everything outside it.

Capacity: The maximum volume that a container can hold. It is measured in special units such as pints or liters.

Circumference: The perimeter of a circle. In Latin *circum* means "around" and "-ference" comes from a word meaning "carrying."

Cubic unit: The same volume as is contained in a unit cube. It can be any shape.

Cuboid: A 3D shape with six faces that are all rectangles; some but not all may be squares.

Degree: A small part of a complete turn. There are 360 degrees in a complete turn.

Diameter: The size of a circle measured straight across through its center. In Greek *dia* means "through" and *metria* means "measurement."

Equation: A number sentence using the = symbol, telling us that two different ways of writing a number are the same. For example, $2 + 2 = 4$ and $9 - 5 = 4$.

Formula: A rule for calculating something. It is often an equation containing a letter or several letters.

Isosceles: A triangle or a trapezium with just two sides the same length is called isosceles.

Pair: Two things that match up in some way.

Parallel: Parallel lines are lines that remain the same distance apart forever.

Perimeter: The size of the boundary of a flat object. It is the distance once around it. In Greek *peri* means "around" and *metria* means "measurement."

Periphery: Another word for circumference.

Perpendicular: Two lines that meet or cross at right angles are called perpendicular.

Pi: The number of times bigger the circumference of a circle is than the diameter. It is given a special name because it cannot be written down precisely as a fraction or as a decimal. It is approximately $^{22}/_7$, or 3.14159265....

Radius: The distance from the center of a circle to its boundary. It is half the diameter. In Latin *radius* means a "ray" or "wheel spoke."

Rectangle: A four-sided shape in which pairs of opposite sides are the same length, and all four corners are right angles.

Right angle: An angle that is exactly a quarter of a complete turn.

Square: A regular rectangle with all four sides the same length and four angles of equal size.

Square unit: The same area as is in a square with sides one unit long. It can be any shape.

Three-dimensional (3D): A three-dimensional shape (3D) has length and breadth and thickness (depth). It can be solid, just a surface, or even an open framework, like a pylon.

Volume: The size of a 3D shape. It is measured in cubic units (such as cm^3 or in^3) by counting how many unit cubes can be fitted into it. *See* Capacity.

Set index